The Big Book of Bible People

Mark Water
Illustrated by
Graham Round

ISBN 1 85608 204 0

Originally published 1996

In Australia this book is published by:
Hunt & Thorpe Australia Pty Ltd.,
9 Euston Street, Rydalmere NSW 2116

A CIP catalogue record for this book is available from the British Library.

Manufactured in Malaysia

CONTENTS

1 ABRAHAM AND SARAH

Haran

From Ur

Terah, Abraham's dad
Terah's claim to fame was his son—Abraham. Terah was born in Ur. He traveled with Abraham to Haran, about 700 miles away. There he died, at age 205. (See Genesis 11:24–32.)

Abraham on the move
When Abraham was 75, his life turned into an adventure. God told him to leave his home in Ur for a new country. He stayed in Haran for a while, and he then set off again with his wife, Sarah, and his nephew, Lot. In Canaan, God said, "I will give you this land forever." Abraham believed God. He traveled in the mountains, living in tents. (See Genesis 12:1–9.)

Beersheba

Lot, rescued from Sodom
At first, Lot lived with Abraham. But their servants kept arguing. Lot moved to the evil city of Sodom. God decided to destroy Sodom, but Abraham prayed for Lot. So God sent two angels to Sodom and they persuaded Lot, his wife, and daughters to escape. (See Genesis 19:1–29.)

Melchizedek, mystery man
Melchizedek met Abraham only once. He was mysterious, "without father, without mother, …having neither beginning of days nor end of life" (Hebrews 7:3). He was king of Jerusalem and "priest of God Most High." He gave Abraham a blessing. (See Genesis 14:18-20; Hebrews 7:1–28.)

Lot's wife
"Hurry!" said the angels. "Get away from Sodom. Do not delay. Do not look back." What did Lot's wife do? She looked back. She got caught in the rain of fire and brimstone and became a pillar of salt. (See Genesis 19:23–26.)

Abram becomes Abraham

God changed Abram's name. When he was born, he was called Abram. When he was 99, God said, "Your name shall be Abraham, for I have made you a father of many nations." (See Genesis 17:5.) *Abraham* means "father of many." Abraham became the founder, or father, of the Jews.

Rebekah, a wife for Isaac

Abraham sent his servant back to Haran to find a wife for Isaac. The servant sat down by a well and prayed, "May the young woman who says, 'Drink, and I will water your camels too,' be the one." Rebekah came out from the town. She was young and beautiful. She offered to get water for all the camels. The servant gave her a gift of jewelry. He found out that she was Abraham's great-niece. When Isaac saw her, he loved her. (See Genesis 24.)

Isaac, the miracle baby

When 90-year-old Sarah heard God say that she would have a son, she laughed. A year later her baby was born. She called him Isaac, which means "he laughs." (See Genesis 21:1–8.)

Hairy Esau and smooth Jacob

Isaac and Rebekah had twin sons. The firstborn was hairy Esau. Jacob wanted the special blessing and right to God's promises that belonged to the firstborn son. He bought the birthright from Esau for a bowl of lentil soup. He got the blessing by dressing up as Esau and tricking his father, who could no longer see. (See Genesis 25:19–34; 27.)

Isaac: a test

Did Abraham love his son Isaac more than he loved God? God gave Abraham a test. He told Abraham to sacrifice Isaac. Abraham built an altar and put wood on it. He was just about to kill Isaac when an angel said, "S T O P!" Abraham had passed the test. Then Abraham saw a ram caught in a bush, and he sacrificed that ram. (See Genesis 22:1–14.)

2 ADAM AND EVE

Adam arrives
God made the universe, planet earth, the land, the sea, animals, birds, and fish. Then He said, "Let Us make human beings in Our image, according to Our likeness." First He made a man, called Adam. Adam was not like the animals. He was a person. He had a soul and could worship God. (See Genesis 1:1–2, 26–27.)

Eve
Adam looked at all the animals and gave them names. But they were not like him. He was lonely. God said, "It is not good that man should be alone." And God made Eve. Eve was "a helper like Adam." (See Genesis 2:18–25.)

The serpent—a sly customer
A serpent came to that garden. He was big trouble. "Can you eat anything you want?" he murmured to Eve. "Yes," she said, "except fruit from the tree in the middle of the garden. If we eat that we will die." "God is telling lies," the serpent lied. "That fruit has the power to make you as wise as God. That is why he does not want you to eat it." (See Genesis 3:1–7.)

Adam and Eve—gardeners
In the East, in Eden, God made a garden. Trees and flowers grew in the garden. Rivers flowed through it. God told Adam and Eve to take care of the garden and all the animals. They ate fruit, nuts, grain, and vegetables. Life in the garden was bliss. (See Genesis 2:8–16.)

Adam and Eve lost their home

You will not believe this, but Adam and Eve let themselves be fooled by the serpent. They decided they knew better than God, and they ate that fruit. That was the start of all the trouble in the world. The garden was no longer a safe place for Adam and Eve. They had to leave. And they had to work hard to make a living. (See Genesis 3:8–24.)

The promise—a "child of Eve"

God did not stop loving Adam and Eve. He made them clothes to wear. And He promised that one day in the future a descendant of Adam and Eve would crush Satan's head. That promise came true when Jesus was born. (See Genesis 3:15, 21; Romans 5:18–19.)

Son No.1: Cain

Adam and Eve's elder son, Cain, murdered his younger brother Abel. When God said, "Where is your brother?" he replied, "I do not know. Am I my brother's keeper?" After that he was a failure as a farmer. No crops would grow for Cain. (See Genesis 4:1–25.)

Son No. 2: Abel

Abel was a shepherd. When it was time to give an offering to God, he gave a lamb. Farmer Cain offered crops. God accepted Abel's offering, but not Cain's. So Cain was already out of step with God. "If you do good I will accept you," God said. But Cain let himself get eaten up with jealousy and hate. (See Genesis 4:1–15.)

Simply the oldest

Nobody will better Methuselah's claim for an entry in the *Guinness Book of World Records* as the longest living person. You would have to be 970 years old to beat him. (See Genesis 5:21–27.)

Son No. 3: Seth

After Cain killed his brother, Seth was born. Eve said, "God has given me another child. He will take the place of Abel." (See Genesis 4:25.)

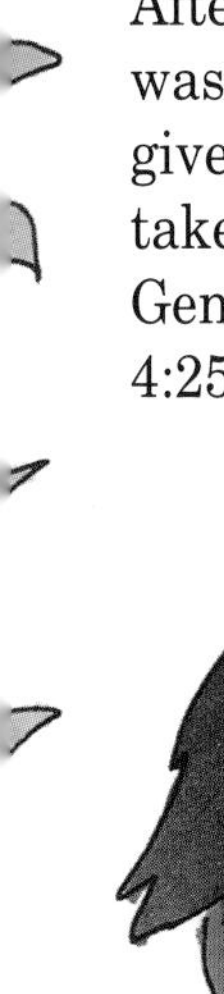

Enoch

One day Enoch went for a walk with God and never came back. "Enoch walked with God. He could not be found because God took him." The only other person in the Bible who went straight to heaven without dying was Elijah.

(See Genesis 5:18–24.)

3 AMOS AND COMPANY

12 "short" prophets
A prophet was someone who spoke up for God. 12 books in the Old Testament are called Minor Prophets. Each one is named after a prophet and gives us his message. *Minor* here means "short."

Obadiah, a very short prophet
Obadiah was writing to the country of Edom. "You want us to suffer," said Obadiah. "But watch out. One day it will be your turn, along with all God's enemies." (See Obadiah.)

Hosea
Hosea's wife left him and their children. Later he came across her. She was up for sale in a slave market. He loved her so much that he bought her back. Hosea's message is that God loves and forgives us like that. (See Hosea 1—3.)

Joel
One summer a horrible plague of locusts swarmed over the land of Judah, gobbling up every bit of food. "They are God's army," Joel said. "They are a sign. People must change their ways." (See Joel 2:1–32.)

Amos
Amos the shepherd took his sheep to the city market. But he did not like what he saw—rich people pretending to be religious while they cheated and made poor people poorer. "God hates what you are doing," he said. For this he got thrown out. (See Amos 1; 5:18–27.)

Jonah
God sent a big fish to rescue Jonah and teach him a big lesson: that God wants to forgive everyone in every country. God loves animals too (look in the last verse of Jonah). (See Jonah 1—4.)

Micah
"Do not think you will escape," Micah thundered to all the evildoers around him. "God is going to destroy all of you." Micah promised that one day a great King would be born in Bethlehem. He would lead His people to safety again like a shepherd. (See Micah 5:2, 4.)

Nahum
The evil city of Nineveh has bitten the dust. Hurrah! said Nahum. (See Nahum 1—3.)

Habakkuk
"It is not fair!" Habakkuk said to God. God answered. Habakkuk came up with a different grumble. God answered again. In the end Habakkuk said he would trust God and be cheerful, no matter what went wrong. (See Habakkuk 1—2.)

Zephaniah
Zephaniah was an aristocrat, descended from King Hezekiah. A horrible time is ahead of us, he said, "darkness and gloom, clouds and blackness." Judgment Day. But he added that, when God had done away with evil, happiness would come again. (See Zephaniah 1:1, 15;

Haggai
"You are having a hard time," Haggai said, "because you are living in fine houses and do not care that God's temple is in ruins." (See Haggai 1:1–8.)

Zechariah
Zechariah backed up Haggai. He urged the people to rebuild the ruined temple. He was a visionary. He saw a great future for God's people. Zechariah promised that one day a King (Jesus) would ride into Jerusalem on a donkey. (See Zechariah 9:9.)

Malachi
This book is the last one in the Old Testament, written about 450 years before Jesus was born. "God's victory is coming," Malachi said. "The prophet Elijah will reappear and lead the way." (See Malachi 4:1–6.)

4 CHILDREN AND YOUNG PEOPLE

Miriam, baby Moses' big sister
"We are not going to let them kill Moses," Miriam said. She helped to make a basket boat and hid it in the reeds in the river. Then she kept watch. The princess of Egypt found the baby. Miriam said, "Shall I get you a nanny for him?" Moses was safe. His own mother looked after him, thanks to Miriam's quick thinking. (See Exodus 2:1–10.)

Samuel and his mother, Hannah
Hannah was sad. "Please, please, let me have a baby," she kept praying to God. "I will not expect him to help me. He can work full time for You." Samuel was born—the happiest day of Hannah's life. When Samuel was old enough, Hannah took him to Eli the priest. He helped Eli in God's worship tent. (See 1 Samuel 1.)

Samuel and the voice in the night
"Samuel!" The voice woke Samuel up. Samuel thought it was Eli. He ran to the priest. "Here I am." But it was not Eli. Three times the voice called. At last Eli got the message. "Go back to bed," Eli said, "and if the voice calls again, say, 'Speak, LORD, I am Your servant and I am listening.'" (See 1 Samuel 3:1–21. For more about Samuel, turn to the page on David.)

A girl who was a servant
She was a little foreign servant girl. He was Naaman, the great army commander, Naaman the brave, Naaman the man with leprosy. The servant girl said to her mistress, "The prophet who lives in my country would heal Naaman." Full of hope, Naaman set off. (See 2 Kings 5:1–3. To find out what happened and to see how Naaman swallowed his pride and got a dunking, turn to Elijah and Elisha.)

Lost
When Jesus was 12, His parents lost Him in Jerusalem. For three days they searched high and low, frantic with worry. At last they found Him in the temple. "Why did You do this to us?" His mother asked. But Jesus said, "Surely you knew I would be here in My Father's house?"
(See Luke 2:41–50.)

Eutychus yawns
On and on and on Paul preached. The upstairs room was crowded. The lamps made the room hot. Eutychus fell fast asleep. Crash! He tumbled out of the open window to the ground three floors below. He was dead. Paul went down and put his arms around the young man. "Do not worry," Paul said. "He is alive now."
(See Acts 20:7–12.)

John Mark
"A young man, wearing only a linen cloth, was following Jesus. The people grabbed him. But the cloth he was wearing came off, and he ran away naked." Only Mark's gospel tells us this tiny story from the night Jesus was arrested. (See Mark 14:51–52.)

5 DANIEL AND HIS FRIENDS

Ashpenaz, Lord High Chamberlain
"They are the pick of the bunch," Ashpenaz said to King Nebuchadnezzar. "We have here the brightest and best young men in all Jerusalem." "Good," said the king to his servant. "Take them back to my palace." Daniel and his friends left Jerusalem forever. (See Daniel 2:1–2.)

Daniel's further education
Daniel, Shadrach, Meshach, and Abed-Nego were being trained to be wise men in King Nebuchadnezzar's palace.
The training course lasted three years. (See Daniel 1:3–7.)

Graduation
After three years all the young men came before King Nebuchadnezzar. He gave them an oral examination. The star pupils were Daniel and his friends. Daniel was good at explaining dreams.
(See Daniel 1:17–21.)

Daniel's diet
On the first day they sat down to a royal feast. "This food is against our law," Daniel said. "If you do not eat it," Ashpenaz said, "you will not be as strong as the others and I will lose my head." Daniel said, "Give us vegetables and water for ten days and then examine us." Ten days later Daniel and his friends were tops in the fitness test.
(See Daniel 1:11–16.)

King Nebuchadnezzar's dream
"I demand to know what my dream means!" the king bellowed to his fortune-tellers, wizards, magicians, and wise men. "O king, live forever!" they said. "First, tell us the dream." The king lost his temper. "They are all impostors. Kill them." But Daniel told the king the dream and its meaning. So Nebuchadnezzar put Daniel in charge of all the wise men.
(See Daniel 2.)

Shadrach, Meshach, and Abed-Nego
It was a great golden statue. "Worship it!" King Nebuchadnezzar ordered. Shadrach, Meshach, and Abed-Nego refused. The king was raging mad. "Heat up the furnace. Throw them in." He sat down to watch them burn up. Then he leaped to his feet. "Look!" he yelled. "Four men walking around. Their God has sent an angel to save them." (See Daniel 3.)

Belshazzar's feast and God's graffiti

After Nebuchadnezzar came King Belshazzar. One day he had a big party. The guests were drinking from gold cups stolen from the temple in Jerusalem. They were singing the praises of idols. Suddenly, Belshazzar's face turned white and his knees knocked together. A disembodied hand was writing words on his palace wall. (See Daniel 5:1–6.)

MENE, MENE, TEKEL, UPHARSIN

This was the writing on the wall. Daniel was summoned. He said, "It means your days are numbered. God has weighed you and found you not good enough. Your kingdom will be split up." Belshazzar put a gold chain around Daniel's neck and made him the third ruler in the kingdom. But that night the king died. (See Daniel 5:7–31.)

The plot

After Belshazzar came King Darius. He put Daniel in charge of his kingdom. All the king's officials were eaten up with jealousy. They hatched a plot to get rid of Daniel. "O king," they said, "make a law that for thirty days anyone who prays to any god except you shall be thrown to the lions." The law was passed. (See Daniel 6:1–16.)

The lions' den

Daniel prayed in front of his window. Then the king saw the trick. But it was too late. "May your God save you," he said as Daniel was thrown into the den. The king spent a sleepless night. Next morning he rushed back and asked, "Has your God been able to save you?" "O king," Daniel called, "an angel of God closed the lions' mouths." Then Darius made a new law: everyone must worship Daniel's God. (See Daniel 6:17–28.)

6 DAVID

Samuel the kingmaker and Saul

Saul was the first king. He was made king when Samuel poured oil on his head. He was head and shoulders taller than all other young men, good-looking, and a good soldier. But he got too proud. He had bad moods and stopped trusting God. So God left him, and Saul did not even know it.
(See 1 Samuel 10; 15.)

David, a shepherd boy

"Stop crying for Saul," God said to Samuel. "Go to Bethlehem. I have chosen one of the sons of Jesse." They lined up. A good-looking bunch. Which one? "I do not judge by appearances," God said. The new king turned out to be David, the kid brother. They had left him with the sheep. It was a secret anointing. David had a long wait ahead of him.
(See 1 Samuel 16:1–13.)

Goliath the giant

He was over nine feet tall. King Saul's soldiers looked at his helmet, bronze armor, and massive spear— and quaked. Goliath was disgusted when he saw young David with a sling. "I will feed your body to the birds," he sneered just before he went crashing to the ground.
(See 1 Samuel 17:1–49.)

David the musician
David was a poet and a musician. When King Saul was in a bad mood, David played his small harp. This calmed the king down. Many of our psalms were written by David. (See 1 Samuel 16:21–23; Psalm 23.)

Michal, King Saul's daughter
Michal fell in love with David, and they were married. Saul was jealous of David and he sent men to kill him. Michal found out. "Hurry," she said. She put an idol in the bed, covered it up, and stuck goat's hair on its head. David climbed out of the window and got away. (See 1 Samuel 19:11–17.)

Jonathan, King Saul's son
Jonathan was a great warrior. He was also David's best friend. They made a pact of lifelong friendship. He was never jealous of David and he helped David escape from Saul. Jonathan knew David's hiding place but never betrayed him. Jonathan and Saul were killed in battle. (See 1 Samuel 20; 2 Samuel 1.)

King David
After Saul died, David became king. He captured Jerusalem and made it his capital city. He was the greatest king Israel ever had. (See 1 Samuel 5:1–12.)

Abigail
David was an outlaw, a Robin Hood, on the run from Saul. Abigail's husband, Nabal, was a rich, mean-spirited man. When David's men needed food, Nabal refused to help. So Abigail piled food and drink onto her donkeys and took it all to David. A few days later Nabal died. David and Abigail were married. (In those days men had more than one wife.) (See 1 Samuel 25.)

Absalom
Prince Absalom, David's son, had a grudge against his dad. He turned the people against David. He wanted to be king. Absalom was galloping through the woods on his mule when his hair got caught in some branches. His mule ran on and he was left dangling in the air. Joab, David's army commander, killed Absalom. (See 2 Samuel 18.)

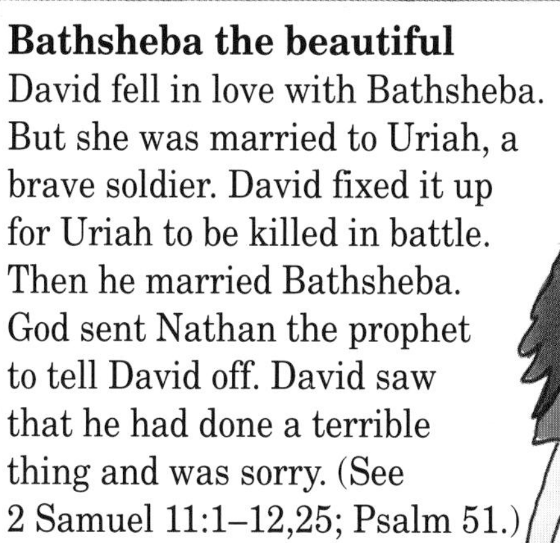

Bathsheba the beautiful
David fell in love with Bathsheba. But she was married to Uriah, a brave soldier. David fixed it up for Uriah to be killed in battle. Then he married Bathsheba. God sent Nathan the prophet to tell David off. David saw that he had done a terrible thing and was sorry. (See 2 Samuel 11:1–12,25; Psalm 51.)

Mephibosheth
Mephibosheth, Jonathan's son, had a disability. In memory of his friend Jonathan, David asked Mephibosheth to live with him in his palace. (See 2 Samuel 9.)

7 ELIJAH AND ELISHA

Ahab and Jezebel
King Ahab married Jezebel, a foreign princess. That was his undoing. Jezebel wanted to make everyone worship Baal. Baal was a nature god. He was supposed to control the weather. Jezebel and all her hundreds of false prophets were made to look stupid by one man: the prophet Elijah in his hairy cloak and leather belt. (See 1 Kings 16:29–33; 2 Kings 1:8.)

Flying delivery service
Elijah said to Ahab, "There will be no rain until I say." Then he went into hiding. He drank water from a small brook. Ravens were his waiters. Twice a day they brought him bread and meat. (See 1 Kings 17:1–6.)

The widow from Zarephath
God told Elijah to stay with a widow and her son. "Please give me some bread," he said. "Sir," she said, "I have only a handful of flour and a few drops of oil." Elijah said, "Make me a loaf and then one for yourself. As long as the drought lasts you will have flour in your bin and oil in your jar." (See 1 Kings 17:8–16.)

Elijah versus the prophets of Baal
It was showdown time on Mount Carmel. "The true God is the God who will send fire to burn up the sacrifice on the altar," Elijah said. The prophets of Baal pranced around chanting. It was no use. Then Elijah prayed. Down came fire from heaven.
(See 1 Kings 18.)

Earthquake, fire, or whisper?
"I will murder Elijah," Jezebel vowed. Elijah ran away. He sank into gloom. He felt he was the only person left who cared about God. He crept into a mountain cave. An earthquake shook the mountain. Fire raged. Then the sense of God's closeness came in a gentle whisper, and God Himself cheered Elijah up. "Now, go back," God said. "Appoint Elisha to help you." (See 1 Kings 19.)

Elijah and the whirlwind
Elijah was nothing if not dramatic. Instead of quietly dying in the normal way, he "went up by a whirlwind into heaven." One minute Elijah and his friend Elisha were walking by the river, and the next minute there was a chariot of fire, with horses of fire, and Elijah had gone up with it into heaven!
(See 2 Kings 2:1–16.)

A miracle
Elisha was told that the son of the widow of Shunem had died. Elisha went to the dead boy's bed and prayed to the Lord. Then the boy sneezed and came to life. (See 2 Kings 4:8–37.)

Naaman, the general with leprosy
The chariot and horses halted outside Elisha's house. The great General Naaman strode to the door. Elisha sent a message: "Wash seven times in the river Jordan." Naaman was furious. "How dare he dismiss me like this! Why does he not wave his hands over me?" Huffing and puffing, Naaman was driven to the river. There God healed him.
(See 2 Kings 5:1–14.)

Gehazi the greedy
"What a terrible waste," Gehazi muttered greedily. "Elisha has refused Naaman's gifts. All that lovely silver and gold." He raced after Naaman. "My master has changed his mind." Naaman gave silver and rich clothes to Gehazi. Gehazi had them in his house, but he could not deceive Elisha. From then on Gehazi had leprosy. (See 2 Kings 5:15–27.)

An invisible army
It was war. "Help! We are trapped," Elisha's servant said one morning. The town was surrounded by enemy soldiers and chariots. But Elisha said, "The army that fights for us is larger than the one against us." Then he prayed, "LORD, open my servant's eyes." The servant looked again, "and he saw that the mountain was full of horses and chariots of fire." It was God's army.
(See 2 Kings 6:14–17.)

8 ESTHER

Esther
There is one book in the Bible that never mentions God or prayer—not even once. That is the book of Esther, named after Esther, queen of Persia. In Persia in those days Jews and their God were often not well liked. It was best to be careful what you said. But in Esther's story we see God at work. And Esther, loyal to God, saved her people from destruction. (See Esther 9:1–32.)

Queen Vashti dares to disobey
King Xerxes was not a man to do things by halves. He put on a banquet that lasted seven days. Wine was served in goblets of gold to people who sat on couches of gold and silver. All went well until King Xerxes commanded Queen Vashti, "wearing her royal crown in order to display her beauty to the people and the nobles," to come in. Queen Vashti refused. That was the end of her. (See Esther 1:4–12.)

Esther and the beauty contest
It was some beauty contest. The winner was to be the next queen. There was a yearlong beauty treatment: six months with oil of myrrh and six months with perfumes and cosmetics. A Jewish orphan girl won. Her name was Esther. (See Esther 2:1–18.)

Mordecai uncovers a plot
Esther had been brought up by her uncle, Mordecai. One day Mordecai overheard two men plotting to kill King Xerxes. He told Esther and she told the king. The two men were hanged. These events were recorded in the court records. (See Esther 2:19–23.)

Haman
Haman was chief adviser to King Xerxes. Everyone had to bow down to him. When Mordecai refused, Haman was really mad! "I will get rid of that Jew," he said. His plot was simple and devastating. He bribed King Xerxes to sign an order that every single Jew in the empire should be killed. (King Xerxes did not know that Esther was a Jew too.) (See Esther 3.)

The gallows

Haman built a gallows 75 feet high in his garden. "This is for Mordecai," Haman said, rubbing his hands in glee. (See Esther 5:9–14.)

A dangerous mission

"You must save us," Mordecai said to Esther. "You must plead with the king. Maybe you were queen for this very reason." But anyone who went to see the king without being called risked being killed. Even Esther. And she had not been called for weeks. "I will go to the king, and if I perish, I perish!" she said. She put on her most beautiful royal robes. (See Esther 4:1–17.)

The counterplan

A miracle! The king was glad to see Esther. She invited the king to a great banquet two nights in a row. On the second night she invited Haman. When the king was full of good food and drink, he said, "I will give you anything you want, up to half my kingdom." "Let me and my people live," she said. And she told the king what Haman had done. (See Esther 5:1–8; 7:1–10.)

A sleepless night

The next night Xerxes could not sleep. "Read the court records to me," he said to his servant. "That will send me to sleep." The servant read how Mordecai had saved the king's life. Mordecai must be honored, said the king to Haman. Haman began to feel afraid. Things were going wrong for him. (See Esther 6:1–10.)

The end of Haman

Haman was hanged on the gallows he had built for Mordecai. Mordecai was given Haman's job. And the king sent out an order saying that the Jews could defend themselves if they were attacked. (See Esther 8.)

9 EZEKIEL

Buzi was my dad
Ezekiel the prophet has one of the longest books of the Old Testament (48 chapters) named after him. His dad, Buzi by name, was a priest who served God in the temple in Jerusalem.
(See Ezekiel 1:3.)

King Nebuchadnezzar invades
When King Nebuchadnezzar captured Jerusalem in 597 B.C., Ezekiel went into exile to Babylon. It was far away from the temple where he wanted to be a priest. "Nebuchadnezzar carried into captivity all Jerusalem: all the captains and mighty men of valor, and all the craftsmen and artisans—a total of ten thousand."
(See 2 Kings 24:8–17.)

Ezekiel by the Chebar River
Ezekiel's job was to encourage God's people who had lost their land, their temple, their king, and their hope. It was while Ezekiel was with the exiles by the Chebar River that he "saw visions of God."
(See Ezekiel 1:1–3.)

Ezekiel's vision of God
Ezekiel saw four angel-like creatures, cherubim. Each one had four faces: a man, a lion, an ox, and an eagle. Their wings touched and so formed a square shape. Through these visions Ezekiel taught the sad exiles that God was still with them.
(See Ezekiel 1:4–28.)

Ezekiel cuts his hair off
One day Ezekiel was told to "take a sharp sword and use it as a barber's razor to shave your head and your beard. Then take a set of scales to divide up the hair." (See Ezekiel 5:1–6.)

Ezekiel and the Shepherd
Ezekiel had a great message of hope for the depressed exiles. God would be like a shepherd to them: "As a shepherd looks after his scattered flock when he is with them, so will I look after My sheep." And best of all, "I will bring them to their own land." (See Ezekiel 34:11–16.)

Scattered hair
Ezekiel was told to scatter a third of his hair to the wind. Through these dramatic actions Ezekiel was teaching God's people that the fall of Jerusalem was God's judgment on their evil ways. (See Ezekiel 5:2–17.)

Ezekiel and the valley of dry bones
God's people exiled in Babylon must have felt like a lot of dry bones. They thought God practically lived in the temple in Jerusalem. In Ezekiel's stunning vision of dry bones coming to life with God's breath and Spirit, the exiles saw a picture of themselves coming alive to God again. (See Ezekiel 37:1–14.)

10 EZRA AND NEHEMIAH

Three cheers for King Cyrus

God sometimes uses the most unlikely people to help His followers. King Cyrus was the mighty king of Persia. Persia became the number one world power after the Babylonians were crushed. This king helped the Jews return to their beloved Jerusalem. (See Ezra 1:1.)

Cyrus and his decree

King Cyrus decreed, "All the kingdoms of the earth the LORD, God of heaven has given me. And He has commanded me to build a temple for Him at Jerusalem in Judah. Any of His people among you may go to Jerusalem to build this temple."
(See Ezra 1:2–4.)

1,000 silver platters

King Cyrus made sure that the exiles of Jerusalem did not return empty-handed. He gave back some of what had been taken from the temple:

- 30 gold platters
- 1,000 silver platters
- 30 gold bowls
- 410 matching silver bowls

The whole lot came to a total of 5,400 articles of gold and silver.
(See Ezra 1:5–11.)

6,720 donkeys

King Cyrus did not forget the animals. He allowed 736 horses, 245 mules, 435 camels, and 6,720 donkeys to return. There were 42,360 people, not to mention 7,337 servants, so there were not enough animals to ride on.
(See Ezra 2.)

Ezra reads the Law

When Ezra the scribe returned to Jerusalem, he wanted everyone to listen to and obey God's commands. So he read the Book of the Law to them for six hours—"from morning until midday." (See Nehemiah 8.)

Sanballat the bully

As soon as Nehemiah arrived in Jerusalem to rebuild its walls and its temple, Sanballat made fun of him. He taunted, "What are these feeble Jews doing? Will they restore the wall? Will they offer sacrifices? Will they complete it in a day? Will they bring the stones back to life from these heaps of rubble—stones that are burned?" (See Nehemiah 4:1–2.)

Nehemiah's donkey ride

When Nehemiah arrived in Jerusalem, he climbed onto his donkey and inspected the walls of Jerusalem. He found the walls were in ruins and the gates had been burned. (See Nehemiah 2:11–20.)

Tobiah plots with Sanballat

Tobiah joined Sanballat and said, "Whatever they build if even a fox goes up on it, he will break down their stone wall." Together they plotted "to come and attack Jerusalem and stir up trouble against it." (See Nehemiah 4:3–9.)

Nehemiah finishes the walls

It took Nehemiah just 52 days to finish rebuilding the walls of Jerusalem. All the people joined in. Nehemiah kept on praying for God's help. And even Tobiah and Sanballat "realized that this work was done with the help of God." (See Nehemiah 6:15–19.)

Two-choir procession

At the dedication of the wall of Jerusalem, Nehemiah had "two large choirs to give thanks." One went on the top of the wall to the right, while the second one went in the other direction. They sang along with the cymbals, harps, lyres, and trumpets. (See Nehemiah 12:27–47.)

11 GIDEON, SAMSON, AND THE JUDGES

Judge Othniel and his victory

The people who ruled over Israel before they had kings were called judges. They were usually either very good and faithful to God or very bad and unfaithful to God. Judge Othniel was a good judge. He gave Israel peace for 40 years. (See Judges 3:9–11.)

The left-handed Judge Ehud

The days of the judges were brutal days. Eglon, king of Moab, had power over Israel, so the left-handed Ehud was sent to him. "Now Ehud made a double-edged dagger about a foot and a half long, and he fastened it under his clothes on his right thigh. Ehud reached with his left hand, took the dagger from his right thigh, and thrust it into Eglon's belly." (See Judges 3:12–30.)

Judge Shamgar defeats the Philistines

Judge Shamgar used an ox goad to kill 600 Philistines. And so he saved Israel. (See Judges 3:31.)

Deborah

Deborah was a prophetess as well as a judge over Israel. In a battle against the Israelites, the Canaanites were defeated. But the commander, Sisera, fled. An Israelite woman, Jael, drove a tent peg through his head as he slept. (See Judges 4–5.)

Gideon and his 300 men
Gideon had a 30,000-man army to fight the Midianites. God said that was too many. So Gideon reduced his army to 300 men. Gideon won. And he also learned the lesson that God's power rather than thousands of soldiers had defeated the Midianites. (See Judges 6—7.)

Abimelech the brutal
After Gideon's death Abimelech became Israel's next judge. He seized the throne by killing 70 out of his 71 brothers. But Abimelech lasted only three years before "a woman dropped an upper millstone on his head and crushed his skull." (See Judges 9.)

Samson the strong
Samson was Israel's most famous judge. He is remembered for his great strength. He once killed 1,000 men with a donkey's jawbone. (See Judges 13—15.)

Samson the weak
Samson's fatal weakness was Delilah. He even told her the secret of his strength—his long hair. He had taken a vow as a Nazirite not to have his hair cut. Once it was cut his strength left him. (See Judges 16.)

12 ISAIAH

Amoz, Isaiah's dad
Isaiah the prophet spoke God's messages to the people of Judah during the reigns of four kings: Uzziah, Jotham, Ahaz, and Hezekiah. Isaiah's dad, no relation of the prophet Amos, was called Amoz. (See Isaiah 1:1.)

Isaiah becomes a prophet
Isaiah became a prophet in a most spectacular way. He had an amazing vision of God's glory (plus six-winged seraphim) filling the temple and God Himself sitting on the throne in the temple. (See Isaiah 6:1–13.)

Isaiah's son, Maher-Shalal-Hash-Baz
What a mouthful: Maher-Shalal-Hash-Baz! God gave Isaiah's son this symbolic name, which meant "quick to the plunder." God was saying that the king of Assyria would attack and defeat the Israelites with great speed. (See Isaiah 8:1–4.)

King Uzziah of Judah
King at 16! Uzziah became king as a teenager, and he ruled for 52 years. Because he tried to offer incense in the wrong way God made him a leper. He had to live in a separate house all by himself. (See 2 Kings 15:1–7.)

King Ahaz of Judah
Uzziah's grandson, Ahaz, did not follow God's ways. However, Isaiah helped Ahaz. When Jerusalem was attacked by Rezin and Pekah, Isaiah assured Ahaz that he would win—which he did. (See Isaiah 7:1–9.)

Hezekiah and his tunnel
Hezekiah, Judah's thirteenth king, had a secret tunnel built. It went from inside Jerusalem, under the city, to a spring of water outside the city. So when Jerusalem was surrounded by armies, the people still had a water supply.
(See 2 Kings 20;
2 Chronicles 32:30.)

Sennacherib
Sennacherib, the mighty king of Assyria, surrounded Jerusalem with his army. But Isaiah told him to surrender. Then a most mysterious thing happened. "The angel of the LORD went to the Assyrian camp and killed 185,000 soldiers. At dawn the next day there they lay—all dead!" (See Isaiah 36—37.)

A suffering servant
Chapter 53 of Isaiah's book has many prophecies that Jesus fulfilled hundreds of years later. When Isaiah wrote, "He was despised and rejected. He has borne our griefs and carried our sorrows. Because of our sins He was wounded. He was buried with the rich," it was as if he saw Jesus dying and being buried.
(See Isaiah 52:12—53:12.)

13 JEREMIAH

Jeremiah—the weeping prophet

Jeremiah had a lot to cry about. For a start, the people in Judah kept doing the exact opposite of what God wanted. So God was sending their enemy the Babylonians to conquer them. Jeremiah said, "Give in to the Babylonians." "Traitor!" everyone jeered. They kept beating him up and putting him in prison or in the stocks. (See Jeremiah 4:19; 20:1–2; 27:12.)

King Josiah of Judah

- At 8 years old: made king
- At 16 years old: began to obey God
- At 20 years old: got rid of all idol worship
- At 21 years old: his friend Jeremiah became a prophet
- At 26 years old: gave orders for the temple to be repaired. The workmen found an old scroll. It was God's long-lost Book of the Law. Josiah read it to all the people
- At 39 years old: killed in battle by an arrow

Everyone was devastated, especially Jeremiah. "Jeremiah wrote some sad songs about Josiah" (See 2 Chronicles 35:25.) (See Jeremiah 22:15–16.)

Jeremiah's call to be a prophet

When the Lord told Jeremiah that he would be a prophet to the nation, Jeremiah complained: "I don't know how to speak; I am only a child." The Lord told Jeremiah: "You must say what I tell you. Do not be afraid. I am with you to rescue you." (See Jeremiah 1:4–10.)

King Jehoiakim of Judah

King Jehoiakim was Josiah's evil son. Jeremiah dictated his sermons to Baruch. When the scroll was read to the king, he was really angry. He hacked it up and burned it on the fire. Jeremiah and Baruch went into hiding, and they wrote it all out again with a lot more added. (See Jeremiah 22:17; 36:1–32.)

Jeremiah has a pottery lesson

"Go down to the potter's house," said God. Jeremiah watched the potter. He was making a clay pot on his wheel. It went wrong. Whoops! He started again, shaping the pot with his hands. God said to Jeremiah, "Cannot I do the same with the people in this country?" (See Jeremiah 18:2–6)

Jeremiah and Baruch

Baruch was Jeremiah's trusty friend and secretary. He stuck it out with Jeremiah in all his trials. "I am tired because of my suffering," Baruch moaned. Jeremiah gave Baruch God's message: "Baruch, you are looking for great things for yourself. Do not do that. I will bring disaster. But I will let you escape alive." (See Jeremiah 45:1–5.)

Jeremiah in the real estate business

When everything was at its blackest, when Babylonian troops were outside Jerusalem, Jeremiah bought a field! It was out in the country, now enemy territory. "One day you will be free again," he said. This is not the end. God says, "I will make a new agreement with the people. All people will know Me. I will remember their sin no more." (See Jeremiah 32:1–15; 31:31–34.)

Enter Ebed-Melech

"It is useless to fight," Jeremiah kept saying. The officers said, "Help! The soldiers are listening!" They dumped Jeremiah into a very deep dungeon. He sank into mud. "That is the end of him." But Ebed-Melech heard about what happened. He lowered down old rags tied to ropes. "Put the rags under your arms," he said. Then he hauled Jeremiah up again. (See Jeremiah 38:1–13.)

Nebuchadnezzar the all-powerful

King Nebuchadnezzar of Babylon strode into Jerusalem. He set fire to the city. He killed a lot of people and herded everyone else off to Babylon. Only the very poorest were left. But he set Jeremiah free. Ebed-Melech and Baruch were safe too. (See Jeremiah 39—40. For more about Nebuchadnezzar see *Daniel*.)

14 JESUS

Jesus
The meaning behind Jesus' sinless life, revolutionary teaching, many miracles, uncontested execution, and extraordinary resurrection lies in His names. He was the Savior of the world, the Son of God, the King of kings, and the Good Shepherd. He once said about Himself, "The Son of Man came to give His life to redeem many people." (See Mark 10:45.)

Joseph
Joseph was Jesus' foster father. Whatever God told Joseph to do he did. God kept on speaking to Joseph in dreams. In a dream Joseph was told

1. that Mary would have a son called Jesus
2. to escape from King Herod to Egypt
3. to go to Nazareth with the baby Jesus and Mary after Herod's death.

(See Matthew 1–2.)

Gabriel
As God's special messenger, the angel Gabriel met very interesting people. Gabriel appeared to Daniel, to Mary, and to Zacharias, who was the father of John the Baptist. Luke records Gabriel's most famous meeting: "God sent the angel Gabriel to a city of Galilee named Nazareth, to a girl named Mary." (See Luke 1:26–27.)

Mary
Mary was only a teenager when God told her that she would have a Son through the action of the Holy Spirit. Mary showed her faith in God with her song, the Magnificat, which begins, "My soul praises the Lord, and my spirit has rejoiced in God my Savior." (See Luke 1:26–56.)

Simeon

Simeon longed with all his heart for one special day to arrive. He had been told by the "Holy Spirit that he would not die before he had seen the Lord's promised Messiah." When Jesus, a tiny baby in Mary's arms, came into the temple, Simeon knew that Jesus was the One he had been waiting for. He gave thanks to God and said, "My eyes have seen Your salvation." (See Luke 2:22–32.)

Anna

Anna saw the baby Jesus in the temple on the same day Simeon did. Anna was at least 84 years old. She did not go to church. She lived there: "She never left the temple. She served God with fastings and prayers night and day." (See Luke 2:33–38.)

Herod the Great

Herod was among the most evil kings who ever reigned. "He gave orders to kill all the baby boys in Bethlehem who were two years old and under." And all that because he became so jealous of Jesus after the wise men asked him where the Messiah would be born. (See Matthew 2:16–18.)

Pontius Pilate

Pontius Pilate was the only person who could have Jesus put to death. Although many of the Jewish leaders hated Jesus, they were not allowed to inflict the death penalty. Pilate knew Jesus was innocent and he even said so—in public. But when Pilate heard the crowd say, "If you let Jesus go, you are not the emperor's friend. Kill Him. Crucify Him," Pilate handed Jesus over to be crucified. (See John 19:1–16.)

Barabbas

Barabbas probably never forgot Jesus to his dying day. Having been found guilty of murder, Barabbas was on death row. On the day he was to be executed Pilate released him as the one prisoner pardoned each year. Barabbas knew he was guilty and that Jesus was innocent. Yet Barabbas had been the one freed. (See Mark 15:1–15.)

15 JOB

Job—animal millionaire
He lived about 4,000 years ago in the land of Uz—somewhere in the East. In those days there was no money. Instead of counting dollars, people counted animals. Job had 7,000 sheep, 3,000 camels, 1,000 oxen, and 500 female donkeys. He had many servants. He was the greatest and richest man in his part of the world. (See Job 1:1–3.)

Job—a good guy
No lying. No cheating. No stealing. Job loved God. He was kind to everyone. And he made sure that his seven sons and three daughters lived good lives. (See Job 1:4–5.)

Satan means "accuser"
In heaven God said, "No one else on earth is like Job. He is innocent of any wrong." Satan said, "He is good only because of what he can get out of it." Was Satan right? Was Job good because it paid him to be good? That is not being good. That is being selfish. (See Job 1:6–11.)

A nightmare comes true
God let Satan strip everything from Job. In one day Job lost all his flocks and his servants. All his children died in an accident. The next day his body was covered in hideous sores. His wife said, "Curse God and die." But Job would not. He said, "Should we take only good things from God and not accept trouble?" (See Job 1:12—2:10.)

Job's friends: Eliphaz, Bildad, and Zophar
They heard the news and came to be with him. For seven days and nights they sat on the ground beside him. In silence. In sorrow. Then Job spoke. He did not curse God. But he cursed the day he was born. (See Job 2:11–13.)

A telling off for Job
All his friends muscled in with good advice.
Eliphaz: You must have done something wrong. Be happy now God is correcting you.
Bildad: Your children must have done something wrong.
Zophar: Put away all your sin and God will forgive you.
On and on they went. Fine talk. But it had nothing to do with Job.
(See Job 4—5; 8; 11.)

Job
"You are all telling lies. I am innocent. I appeal to God."
(See Job 13:1–8.)

Elihu
The youngest of Job's friends, Elihu, spoke up when the others ran out of arguments. He took a long time to say that Job was suffering because God wanted to teach him a lesson.
(See Job 32—37.)

A close encounter with God
Then God spoke straight to Job. He showed Job His power. It was awesome. Mind-boggling. Vast oceans. Great sea creatures. Storms. Stars. Fierce animals hunting their prey. Job saw how pathetic and puny he was. He could hardly speak. "I am sorry," he said. "I am vile." (See Job 38—41.)

The end of the story
Satan had been proved wrong. In all his troubles Job had stuck with God. God was angry with Job's friends. They had attacked Job instead of helping him. But God forgave them when Job prayed for them. After that Job's brothers and sisters and all his friends rallied around to help. And God gave Job twice as many animals and servants as he had before. He had children and grandchildren and great-grandchildren. And he was perfectly happy. (See Job 42:7–17.)

16 JOHN THE BAPTIST

Zacharias, John's dad
"Wh-o-o-o-o's there?" said Zacharias, the older priest, in a trembling voice. He was alone in the Holy Place of the great temple. Outside, the people were praying. Inside, in the dim glow of the lamp, as incense swirled above his head, he saw the angel. He was terrified. (See Luke 1:5–12.)

The angel Gabriel
The angel said, "Your prayer is heard. You will have a son, called John. He will lead many people back to God." Zacharias said, "How can I know you are telling the truth?" The angel said, "I am Gabriel. I stand before God. Now you will not be able to speak until the baby is born." That taught Zacharias not to doubt an angel! (See Luke 1:13–24.)

Elizabeth, John's mother
Elizabeth was no longer young. But she found she was pregnant for the first time in her life. She said, "The Lord has taken away my shame." When she was six months pregnant, her cousin Mary visited her from Nazareth. Elizabeth said, "When I heard your voice, the baby inside me jumped for joy."
(See Luke 1:25, 44.)

Dressed for the part
When he was grown up, John went to live by himself in the rocky desert. He wore a camel's hair tunic and cloak tied with a leather belt, like the prophet Elijah hundreds of years earlier. His food was locusts and wild honey. (See Matthew 3:4.)

A warning voice
The news spread like a brushfire: a new preacher. The country had not heard preaching like it since olden days. When people asked who he was, John quoted from the Old Testament. He said he was "a voice crying in the wilderness: 'Prepare the way of the LORD.'"
(See Matthew 3:3.)

John's message
Everybody came to hear John. To all the people he said, "Turn fro n your evil ways. The Deliverer is coming." "You snakes," he said to the religious leaders, "change your lives." To tax collectors he said, "Stop stealing." To soldiers, "Stop bullying." To ordinary people, "Do not be mean." (See Luke 3:7–14.)

John and Jesus
John and Jesus were cousins. John was six months older than Jesus. John baptized people in the river Jordan as a sign that they were sorry for the wrong things they had done. When Jesus came, John had a problem. Jesus had done nothing wrong! John said to Jesus, "You ought to baptize me!" (See Matthew 3:13–15.)

John and King Herod
King Herod married his brother's wife while his brother was still alive. "That is wrong!" John thundered. So Herod threw him in prison. (See Matthew 14:3–4.)

John in prison
Prison! After the wild, free desert, the winds, the night sky. In prison John had doubts. He sent a message to Jesus: "Are You really the One we are expecting?" Jesus said to the people, "John the Baptist is greater than any other man who has ever lived up to now." (See Matthew 11:2–11.)

Herodias
Herodias hated John. She wanted him killed. But Herod Antipas liked listening to John's sermons. And he was afraid to kill such a popular hero. (See Matthew 14:5; Mark 6:20.)

Salome
Salome was Herod Philip and Herodias's daughter. One day Herod Antipas had a wild birthday party. Salome danced in front of him. "What a dance!" he called. "For that I will give you a present—anything." Salome whispered to her mother. Then she called out, "I want John's head on a plate." Everyone heard. Herod Antipas did not want to lose face in front of his guests. "Do it," he ordered his soldiers.
(See Matthew 14:6–12.)

17 JOHN AND JAMES THE APOSTLES

John and James follow Jesus
Peter and Andrew were brothers and fishermen. James and John were brothers and fishermen. They all worked together with James and John's father, Zebedee. One day, Zebedee found himself all alone. Jesus called John and James, and the other brothers, to follow Him. (See Matthew 4:18–22.)

"Sons of Thunder"
Jesus gave James and John a nickname: "Sons of Thunder." Nobody quite knows why. Some people think it may have been because they had quick tempers. The word that Jesus actually used was *Boanerges*. (See Mark 3:13–19.)

John and the Last Supper
For Jesus' last meal on earth, the Last Supper, you can imagine that He would have chosen very carefully which of His disciples sat next to Him. John was given the honor of sitting right next to Jesus. (See John 13:21–29.)

John the gospel writer
John never mentions himself by name in the gospel of John. He refers to himself as "the beloved disciple" or "the one Jesus loved" but never as "John." John also wrote three very short letters that are in the New Testament. No prizes for guessing their names—1 John, 2 John, and 3 John! (See John 21:7.)

John in exile

Many of the first Christians were persecuted or martyred. John ended up in exile on the island of Patmos in the Aegean Sea. It was there that he wrote the book of Revelation. "I was put on the island of Patmos because I had proclaimed God's word." (See Revelation 1:9–11.)

James and the inner three

James never said much in the New Testament, but he was always there, along with Peter and John, as one of Jesus' inner circle of three trusted friends. So James, along with Peter and John, saw Jesus' transfiguration and the healing of Jairus's daughter and Jesus at prayer in the Garden of Gethsemane. (See Mark 5:21–43.)

James the martyr

Stephen was the first Christian martyr and James was the second—thanks to wicked King Herod Agrippa I, ruler of all Palestine. "King Herod began to harass some members of the church. Then he had James, the brother of John, killed with the sword." (See Acts 12:1–2.)

18 JOSEPH

Jacob spoils Joseph
Joseph was the favorite of his dad, Jacob. One day Jacob made the 11 other sons white hot with jealousy. Jacob gave Joseph a coat of many colors. It was actually a robe with long sleeves. (See Genesis 37:1–4.)

Joseph and his dreams
It was not Joseph's fault that he had the kind of dreams that were almost bound to upset his family. In one of his dreams he saw the sun, the moon, and 11 stars bowing down to him. Since Joseph had 11 brothers, it was hardly surprising that his father said, "Do you think that your mother, your brothers, and I are going to bow down to you?" (See Genesis 37:5–11.)

Potiphar gives Joseph a good job
In Egypt Joseph was sold to one of the king's important officials, Potiphar. Joseph was such a loyal hard worker that Potiphar soon handed over everything he had to the care of Joseph. (See Genesis 39:1–6.)

Brother Reuben tries to save Joseph
Some of Joseph's brothers were so jealous that they decided to kill Joseph. Reuben, the eldest of the 12 brothers, suggested that they put him in a well without hurting him. He planned to rescue Joseph later, but by the time he returned the other brothers had sold Joseph to traders. (See Genesis 37:12–36.)

Potiphar's wife gets Joseph into trouble

Joseph was good-looking. Potiphar's wife was attracted to him. So when Joseph refused all her advances, Potiphar's wife saw to it that Joseph ended up in prison. (See Genesis 39:7–23.)

Joseph and the king's dreams

The king had a most disturbing dream. Seven thin cows gobbled up seven fat cows. Nobody could tell him what it meant—until Joseph was sent for. He quickly changed out of prison clothes and told the king, "God has told you what is going to happen. And the fact that you dreamed this dream twice shows that it will definitely happen. There will be seven years of good crops followed by seven years of no crops." (See Genesis 41:1–36.)

Prime Minister Zaphnath-Paaneah

The king was pleased with Joseph and his interpretation of the dream. "The king took his signet ring off his hand and put it on Joseph's hand." In addition Joseph was given a fine linen robe, a gold chain around his neck, and the second-best chariot in the land. (See Genesis 41:37–45.)

Asenath, Joseph's wife

The king of Egypt also gave Joseph a wife, called Asenath. Joseph gave their two sons names with special meanings. His first son he called Manasseh as he remembered that "God has made me forget all my sufferings and all my father's family." And his second son he called Ephraim, thinking that "God has given me children in the land of my trouble." (See Genesis 41:45–52.)

19 JOSHUA

Caleb the positive
Caleb was one of the 12 spies Moses sent to check out the promised land of Canaan. Ten returned with a very negative report: "They are so huge. We look like grasshoppers next to them. Let us not go there." But Caleb said, "We should go up and take the land. We can do it." (See Numbers 13.)

Nun, Joshua's dad
After Moses died, Joshua took over from him and became the commander-in-chief of the Israelites. His father's name was Nun. Joshua's name means "God is salvation." (See Joshua 1:1–4.)

Joshua's motto
Many people have used the words the Lord said to Joshua as a kind of motto for themselves: "Do not be afraid, nor dismayed, for the LORD your God is with you wherever you go." (See Joshua 1:5–9.)

Rahab of Jericho
Joshua sent spies into Jericho. Two would have been caught if it had not been for the quick thinking and kindness of Rahab. "She took the two spies up to her roof and hid them under some stalks of flax." Then she let them down the wall of Jericho. Rahab hung a red cord out of her window as a secret sign, so when the Israelites attacked, Rahab and her family were spared. (See Joshua 2.)

Seven rams' horns defeat Jericho

The Lord gave unusual military instructions to Joshua about how he should capture the town of Jericho: "You and your soldiers, with seven priests carrying rams' horns, are to march around the city wall once a day for six days. On the seventh day march around seven times with the horns blowing. Then they are to sound one long note and all the people are to shout." The wall collapsed! (See Joshua 6.)

Achan and defeat at Ai

Achan decided it was help-yourself time. After the defeat of Jericho, he took a lot of silver, a bit of gold, and a beautiful Babylonian cloak. He thought he would never be found out. But when the Israelites failed to capture the next town of Ai, the sin was traced back to Achan. (See Joshua 7.)

Joshua's sermon

Just before Joshua died, he preached a sermon. Joshua longed for the Jews to love and obey God. So he told them, "Today, choose whom you will serve: the true God of Israel or these other fake gods all around us. As for me and my family we will serve the LORD." The people replied, "We will also serve the LORD. He is our God." (See Joshua 24:1–28.)

20 MARYS, FOUR OF THEM

Mary, who loved to listen to Jesus
Jesus often stayed with Lazarus and his two sisters, Mary and Martha. Jesus loved each of them. Mary's greatest delight was sitting at Jesus' feet and listening to His every word. (See Luke 10:38–39.)

Mary's sister, Martha
Jesus loved Lazarus and his two sisters, Mary and Martha. Martha always made sure all her guests had enough to eat and drink. But she was so keen on being the perfect host that Jesus once told her: "Martha, Martha! You are worried and troubled about many things." Martha knew that she should be more like her sister, Mary. (See Luke 10:40–42.)

Mary, Jesus' mother
When Jesus was born, Mary was most probably in her teens. So when the angel Gabriel surprised Mary with the amazing news that she would be the mother of the Savior of the world, Mary showed her great faith. She humbly said, "I am the Lord's servant. Let it be to me according to your word." (See Luke 1:26–38.)

Mary at the wedding party
A wedding party was in full swing in Cana. Jesus' mother, Mary, was there, as were Jesus and His disciples. Very, very few words of Mary are recorded. On this occasion Mary told the servants there to "do whatever Jesus tells you." That way Mary knew that Jesus would solve the problem of the lack of wine. (See John 2:1–12.)

Mary at Jesus' death
Mary's heart broke as she watched Jesus slowly die on the cross. But Jesus had not forgotten her. To John, Jesus said, "She is your mother." And to Mary, Jesus said, "He is your son." (See John 19:25–27.)

Mary Magdalene: the first person to see Jesus alive
The first person Jesus appeared to after His resurrection was not one of His 12 disciples but a woman! Mary Magdalene. Mary had gone to Jesus' tomb very early on Sunday morning while it was still dark. When Jesus appeared to her, the first word He said was, "Mary!"
(See John 20:1–18.)

Mary Magdalene is healed
Jesus did not travel only with His 12 disciples. We know of at least three women who sometimes traveled with Him: Susanna, Joanna, and Mary Magdalene were their names. Jesus had sent out seven demons from Mary Magdalene.
(See Luke 8:1–3.)

Mary, the mother of James and John
Mary, the wife of Zebedee, the mother of James and John, once asked Jesus to do something that He had no right to do. Mary wanted her two sons to sit at Jesus' right hand and left hand when He became King. Jesus replied, "These places belong to those for whom My Father has prepared them." Jesus went on to say that if you want to be great, you must be everyone's servant. (See Matthew 20:20–28.)

Mary, the mother of John Mark
The mother of Mark, or John Mark, who wrote Mark's gospel, was another Mary. In the days before there were any church buildings, the first Christians met in homes. Mary's house in Jerusalem must have been a big one, because "many were gathered together praying."
(See Acts 12:12–15.)

21 MOSES

Moses in the bulrushes

The Egyptians were out to kill all the Jewish baby boys. So when Moses was three months old his mother made a basket out of reeds and covered it with tar to make it watertight. "She put Moses in it and placed it in the bulrushes at the edge of the river." (See Exodus 2:1–3.)

Older sister Miriam

Moses' older sister, Miriam, stood some distance from the basket to see what would happen. The king's daughter came for a dip and she discovered Moses crying in his basket. A servant went for a Jewish woman to be the baby's nurse. Miriam, who just happened to be standing there, obliged and fetched Moses' mother. (See Exodus 2:4–10.)

Moses and the non-burning burning bush

Moses blinked. He could not believe his eyes. Was it a mirage? There in front of him was a bush on fire which was not burning! As he came closer to it God spoke to him. "Take off your sandals, you are on holy ground. I am going to use you to rescue the Israelites from Egypt." (See Exodus 3:1–10.)

Older brother Aaron

God said to Moses, "Go and speak to Pharaoh." Moses replied, "No, Lord, do not send me, I am a poor speaker. Send someone else." So God chose Moses' older brother Aaron and said to Moses, "You speak to Aaron and tell him what to say." In this way Moses and Aaron became a team. (See Exodus 4:1–17.)

Moses and the ten plagues

The king of Egypt would not free the Israelites, so Moses, through Aaron, told him that God would send various plagues.

1. Water became blood.
2. Frogs jumped everywhere, even in the soup.
3. Gnats and then
4. Flies everywhere.
5. A dreadful disease among animals.
6. An outbreak of boils.
7. Hail, as big as tennis balls.
8. locusts, gobbling anything edible.
9. A frightening darkness.
10. The death of the firstborn.

(See Exodus 7–11.)

Moses and the sea

At last! The Israelites had been allowed to leave their slavery in Egypt. They were on their way. They were just coming up to the Red Sea when they spied the war chariots and army of the Egyptians coming up behind them. Now Moses was in a real fix. The Israelites jeered at Moses, "Did you bring us out here to die?" Moses said, "Do not be afraid! Stand your ground, and you will see what the Lord will do to save you today." The rest is history, how the Red Sea opened up before them, let them through and then went back, covering and drowning the Egyptians. (See Exodus 14.)

Father-in-law Reuel, known as Jethro

Moses had lots of help from his family: Miriam, Aaron, and now from his father-in-law, Jethro. Moses was exhausted. He'd spent all day settling disputes among the people. Jethro watched and gave this advice. "Choose capable men to be leaders of thousands, hundreds, fifties, and tens. Let them be their judges. Only the difficult cases are to be brought to you." (See Exodus 18:13–27.)

The Ten Commandments

On top of Mount Sinai God gave Moses ten rules for living for the Israelites which we now know as the Ten Commandments:

1. Only worship God.
2. Do not make any images of God.
3. Do not use God's name for evil purposes.
4. Keep the Sabbath holy.
5. Respect your mom and dad.
6. Do not murder.
7. Do not commit adultery.
8. Do not steal.
9. Do not accuse anyone falsely.
10. Do not desire what belongs to someone else.

(See Exodus 20:1–17.)

Moses and the holy tent

God told Moses to "make a sacred tent." It wasn't to be any old tent, but was made out of the finest red, purple, and blue wool, with gold hooks and silver bases for the tent poles! It kept the covenant box (which had the Ten Commandments in it) and it was where God met the Israelites. The temple buildings were modeled on this tent. (See Exodus 25—26.)

22 NICODEMUS AND THE RELIGIOUS LEADERS

Nicodemus visits Jesus at night
So why did Nicodemus not meet with Jesus during the day? Was he scared of what the other Pharisees would think if they knew that he had spoken to this way-out teacher? Jesus told Nicodemus to be "born again." And this top religious leader did not have a clue what Jesus meant! (See John 3:1–21.)

Nicodemus speaks up for Jesus
The Pharisees had it in for Jesus. After the guards had failed to arrest Him the Pharisees derided them and said, "Did he fool you too?" But one of the Pharisees surprised everyone as he spoke up for Jesus: "Does our law judge a man before it hears him?" Good for Nicodemus. (See John 7:45–52.)

Nicodemus helps to bury Jesus' body
Nicodemus pops up for a third time in the Gospels. A rich, secret disciple of Jesus, named Joseph of Arimathea, and Nicodemus took the dead body of Jesus from the cross to Joseph's tomb. They used mixed myrrh and aloes as they wrapped the body of Jesus in linen. (See John 19:38–42.)

Caiaphas the high priest
Caiaphas was high priest in Jerusalem from A.D. 18 to A.D. 36. He pronounced Jesus guilty of blasphemy and sent Him back to Herod to be sentenced to death. His attack on Christianity did not end there. Caiaphas was responsible for arresting and imprisoning many of the early Christians, including Peter. (See Matthew 26:3–68; Acts 5:17–42.)

Simon the Pharisee

Jesus accepted Simon's invitation to dinner. Poor Simon. He never expected that "a woman in the city who was a sinner" should then come in and stand behind Jesus. She wet His feet with her tears and then dried His feet with her hair, kissed His feet, and poured perfume on them. Simon was fuming. "Does he not know who this woman is who is touching him?" Jesus replied with a parable and the punch line, "Whoever has been forgiven little shows only a little love." (See Luke 7:36–50.)

Jesus and the Pharisees

The Pharisees were the official religious leaders. They saw Jesus and His teaching as a serious threat to them. They hated crowds of people hanging on Jesus' every word. They became so mad with Jesus that they plotted to kill Him. (See John 11:45–57.)

Jesus and the teachers of the Law

The teachers of the Law (sometimes called scribes or lawyers) wanted everyone to show them respect. They wanted people to call them "Teacher," and Jesus taught, "you must not be called Teacher." They taught "respect to a teacher should exceed respect for a father, for both father and son owe respect to a teacher." Jesus gave this advice to the crowds about teachers of the Law: "Do as they say, not as they do." (See Matthew 23:1–12.)

23 NOAH

Noah and the evil people

There was murder; Cain had killed his brother Abel. There was violence everywhere. Everyone did what was evil in God's sight. As God looked down on the world "He saw that it was evil." (See Genesis 6:1–8, 11–12.)

Noah: a good man

It was not that Noah was a goody-goody. It was just that he aimed to please God in everything he did. "Noah had no faults and was the only good man of his time. He lived in fellowship with God." (See Genesis 6:9–10.)

Mr. Noah builds an ark

"Mr. Noah builds an ark,
The people think it's such a lark!"
chanted Noah's neighbors. Can you imagine? Building a huge floating zoo so far from any sea or river! But Noah did what God told him: "Make yourself an ark of gopherwood."
(See Genesis 6:13–22.)

The ark saves Noah's family

"The rain was on the earth forty days and forty nights." As the waters rose, the ark floated high above the land. Noah and his family, not to mention the wild animals, livestock, insects, and birds, were safe.
(See Genesis 7:1–24.)

Noah and the raven

Bump! All the animals fell over. The ark had come to rest on Mount Ararat. Noah opened the window in the ark and let out a raven. "It kept flying around until the water had gone down." (See Genesis 8:1–7.)

Noah and the doves

"Noah also sent out a dove to see if the water had gone down." But it flew back to the boat and perched on Noah's hand. After seven more days, Noah tried again. This time the dove came back with "a fresh olive leaf." After another seven days, Noah sent out the dove and it never returned. At last! The waters had gone down. (See Genesis 8:3–12.)

Noah and God's special promise

God wanted to reassure Noah that a flood like this would never happen again. So God said, "I have put my rainbow in the clouds as a sign. A flood will never again destroy all living beings." No wonder we love to see the rainbow! (See Genesis 9:1–17.)

Shem, Ham, and Japheth

Noah had three sons: Shem, Ham, and Japheth. With their wives and their mom and dad they were the only humans to survive the Flood. "Eight souls … were saved through water" (1 Peter 3:20). They became the ancestors of all the people on earth. (See Genesis 9:18–19.)

24 PAUL

From Saul to Paul
The bright midday sun was burning down. Saul was off to Damascus to round up Christians and have them put in prison or put to death. Then a light from the sky flashed around him. He fell to the ground and heard a voice saying, "I am Jesus, whom you persecute." This was Saul's big moment. He changed his name from Saul to Paul. He changed from being a persecutor into a preacher. (See Acts 9:1–8.)

Ananias
When Paul arrived in Damascus, he had to be led by the hand because he could not see. God arranged for Ananias to visit Paul. He said, "Brother Saul, Jesus Himself sent me so that you might see again and be filled with the Holy Spirit." Paul's eyesight came back and he was baptized. (See Acts 9:10–19.)

Barnabas
No wonder Barnabas' nickname was "son of encouragement"! The Christians at Jerusalem knew that Paul had had Christians killed and they would not let him join them. In stepped Barnabas. Barnabas spoke up for Paul and explained "how Saul had seen the Lord on the road." Then they all welcomed Paul with open arms. (See Acts 9:26–28.)

Onesimus

Onesimus was a runaway slave. Somehow he met up with Paul, most likely in Rome, and became a follower of Jesus. Paul sent Onesimus back to his master Philemon, who was also a friend of Paul's. But Paul did not send Onesimus back empty-handed. He gave him a letter addressed to Philemon, asking for Philemon to take Onesimus back. (See Philemon.)

Timothy

Timothy's grandmother, Lois, as well as his mother, Eunice, had "genuine faith." Timothy was like a son to Paul. He became the leader of the Christians in Ephesus and Paul sent him two letters (1 Timothy and 2 Timothy) to encourage him.

Silas

Silas helped Paul on his second big missionary tour. He found it hard going. In Philippi, with Paul, he was put in prison and beaten. Later, he helped to write down some of Paul's famous letters to the first Christian churches. (See Acts 15:22—17:15.)

Lydia, the businesswoman

Lydia was a businesswoman who traded by buying and selling cloth. Her specialty was the much-sought-after purple cloth. In Philippi she heard Paul preach, and she became "a true believer in the Lord." (See Acts 16:11–15.)

Priscilla and Aquila

Priscilla and Aquila are a Jewish wife and husband team that Paul met in Corinth. They are mentioned five times in the pages of the New Testament. Paul tells us that they "risked their own necks" for him. (See Romans 16:3–4.)

Dr. Luke

Luke was a man of many talents. He was a doctor (Paul calls him "the beloved physician"), a writer (the author of Luke's gospel), and a traveling companion (once shipwrecked in the bargain), and loyal friend of Paul. (See Colossians 4:14.)

25 PETER

Starts to follow Jesus
Peter was a strong, rugged fisherman. His brother Andrew introduced him to Jesus. Jesus told him to stop catching fish and to start catching people! He "left everything and followed Jesus." (See Luke 5:1–11)

Promises never to desert Jesus
Peter was sad. Jesus had just said that all of His 12 close friends would desert Him in His hour of need. Peter said he would never, never, never do that. "I would rather die than do that," protested Peter. (See Matthew 26:31–35.)

Denies knowing Jesus three times
Jesus predicted that Peter would deny that he knew Jesus three times before the rooster crowed. After Jesus was arrested, Peter was asked three times if he knew Jesus. Each time he denied it. Then the rooster crowed. Peter "went out and cried bitterly." (See Matthew 26:69–75.)

Meets up with the risen Jesus

The risen Lord Jesus met Peter on the shore of Lake Tiberias. Three times Jesus asked Peter, "Do you love Me more than the other disciples?" Three times Peter replied, "Yes." Jesus told him to "feed My sheep." And He also said that Peter would be martyred. Peter knew that he had been forgiven for his three denials of Jesus. (See John 21:15–19.)

Becomes leader of the first Christians

After Jesus had ascended to heaven the Holy Spirit came on the day of Pentecost. That day Peter stepped up as the preacher. The result? About 3,000 people "believed his message and were baptized." (See Acts 2:2–42.)

Aeneas, healed by Peter

On a visit to Lydda, Peter met Aeneas, who had not been able to get out of bed for eight long years. Peter cured his paralysis, and the people of Lydda "turned to the Lord" when they saw Aeneas walking about. (See Acts 9:32–35.)

Dorcas, brought back to life by Peter

Everyone loved Dorcas. She sewed shirts and wove coats, and she "was full of good works and charitable deeds." Then she died. But Peter arrived, went to her room, knelt beside her, and prayed. And Dorcas came back to life! (See Acts 9:36–43.)

Convert Cornelius

Peter never mixed with non-Jews. One day he had a most disturbing dream. It resulted in him calling on Cornelius—a non-Jew—something he would never have done before his dream! Peter preached and then said, "These people have received the Holy Spirit. Can anyone stop them from being baptized?" (See Acts 10.)

26 RUTH

Elimelech of Bethlehem

Elimelech lived in the time of the judges. It was a wild, rough time when lawless people pleased themselves. In the town of Bethlehem there was a famine. Elimelech was not the type to sit back and do nothing. With his wife, Naomi, and two young sons, he went off to the land of Moab. (See Ruth 1:1–3.)

Naomi—from sweet to bitter

Naomi's husband died in Moab but she still had her sons, Mahlon and Chilion. The years passed. The boys grew up and married local girls. Then Mahlon and Chilion both died. Naomi did not want to stay in such a sad place, so she returned home. Back in Bethlehem she said, "Do not call me Naomi [my sweet one]. Call me Mara [bitter]." (See Ruth 1:3–22.)

Orpah, Naomi's daughter-in-law

Orpah and Ruth had married Naomi's sons. Orpah was a childless widow. "I will go back with you to Bethlehem," Orpah said. She set off with Naomi and Ruth. But Bethlehem was a long way off. A foreign land. "Do not come with me," Naomi said. "My life is too sad for you." Crying bitterly, Orpah kissed Naomi good-bye. (See Ruth 1:6–15.)

Ruth and Naomi

"I will never leave you," Ruth said to Naomi. "Every place you go, I will go. Every place you live, I will live. Your people will be my people. Your God will be my God. And where you die, I will die. And there I will be buried." (See Ruth 1:16–17.)

Ruth, a foreigner in Bethlehem

It was April, the beginning of the barley harvest, when Ruth and Naomi arrived in Bethlehem. There were no pensions for penniless widows. What could they do? Ruth went to the barley fields. God's law said that the harvesters must let poor people collect leftover grain from the fields. (See Ruth 2:1–3.)

Enter Boaz, a wealthy man
Ruth went to collect grain in the fields of Boaz, a rich farmer. Boaz was kind. He told Ruth to stay in his fields and to share his servants' food. "Look after Ruth," he said to his servants. That night Ruth went home with lots of grain. Every day Ruth collected grain from Boaz's fields. (See Ruth 2:3–23.)

Boaz and Ruth
Why was Boaz kind to Ruth? Well, he thought it was great of her to stick it out with Naomi. Also he was related to Naomi. It was his duty to help her. At the end of the harvest Naomi said to Ruth, "You should be married. Tonight go down to see Boaz where he is guarding the grain. He will take care of you." (See Ruth 3.)

Boaz falls for Ruth
Boaz wanted to marry Ruth. But there was a snag. There was a closer relative who ought to care for her. Boaz went to the city gate where all the men sat around and made decisions. The other relative did not want to marry Ruth. "Then I will," said Boaz. The relative gave Boaz his sandal. That was their way of shaking hands on a deal. (See Ruth 4.)

Grandmother Naomi
Boaz and Ruth had a baby boy called Obed. Naomi adored him. In those days no one wanted the family name to vanish. God's law stepped in to help. It said that Ruth's first son was counted as dead Elimelech's son. Naomi was not Mara (bitter) any longer. She had her own grandson. (See Ruth 4:13–16.)

King David
When he grew up Obed had a son called Jesse. And Jesse was the father of the great King David. So Ruth was King David's great-grandmother, and Bethlehem came to be called "King David's town." (See Ruth 4:18–22.)

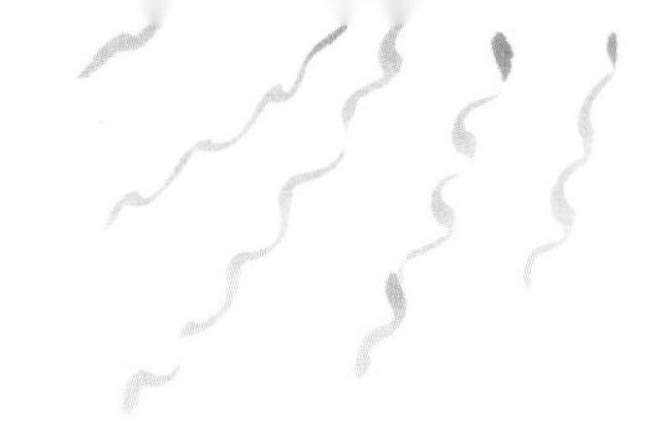

27 SOLOMON

Solomon becomes king
"Solomon was king over all Israel." It was a time of peace and, for Solomon, prosperity. Clearly, Solomon had quite an appetite! "The supplies Solomon needed each day were 180 bushels of fine flour and 360 bushels of meal, ten stall-fed cattle, twenty pasture-fed cattle, and a hundred sheep, besides deer, gazelles, roebucks, and poultry." (See 1 Kings 4:22–23.)

Solomon's temple of gold
Solomon loved building projects. He was the first person to build a temple in Jerusalem for God. He used 80,000 men to quarry the stones for the walls and 70,000 men to carry the stones from the quarry. "The inside of the temple was covered with gold, and gold chains were placed across the entrance of the inner room, which was also covered with gold." (See 1 Kings 5—6.)

Solomon's dream
The Lord spoke to Solomon in a dream and said, "What would you like Me to give you?" Instead of asking for a million dollars, Solomon asked "for wisdom to rule justly." God granted Solomon his wish—and then Solomon woke up. (See 1 Kings 3:1–15.)

Dedication day
As soon as the temple was finished Solomon dedicated it to God, along with 22,000 cattle and 120,000 sheep. Pride of place was given to Solomon's prayer: "Sovereign LORD, look with favor on Your people Israel and hear their prayer whenever they call to You for help." (See 1 Kings 8.)

Solomon and the two mothers

"This baby is mine." "No, he is not, he is mine." Two mothers came to Solomon. Each said a baby boy was hers. How could Solomon decide who the true mother was? He ordered that the baby boy should be cut in two and half given to each mother. One woman agreed to this, but the true mother shouted out, "No, do not kill him. Give him to the other woman." Then Solomon knew who the real mother was, and he ordered the baby to be given to her.
(See 1 Kings 3:16–28.)

The Queen of Sheba visits Solomon

The Queen of Sheba was impressed. When she visited Solomon, she saw his wealth. And it left her "breathless." She had been told that Solomon was wise too. So she "asked Solomon all the questions she could think of. Solomon answered them all."
(See 1 Kings 10:1–8.)

The Queen of Sheba praises God

The queen could not get over Solomon's wisdom and wealth. So she said, "Praise the LORD your God! He has shown how pleased He is with you by making you king of Israel! Because the LORD has loved Israel forever, therefore He made you king, to maintain law and justice." (See 1 Kings 10:9.)

Chaos after Solomon dies

After Solomon died his kingdom did not last. His son Rehoboam could not stop the ten northern tribes from rebelling against him and making Jeroboam their king. That was the beginning of the end of Israel. (See 1 Kings 12–13.)

28 STEPHEN AND THE EARLY CHRISTIANS

Ananias and Sapphira
Ananias and his wife, Sapphira, sold some property and gave the money to the apostles. At least that was what they hoped everyone would think. In reality they kept some of the money back but said that they were giving all the money away. They came to a bad end—they died on the spot. (See Acts 5:1–11.)

Gamaliel, the brave Pharisee
Miracles! Wonders! About 3,000 baptized! The Sadducees could bear no more. They were furious. "They wanted to have the apostles put to death." But one member of the Jewish council, Gamaliel, said, "Leave them alone! If what they do is only human work it will disappear. But if it is from God you will not be able to defeat them." Gamaliel won the day and the apostles were not killed.
(See Acts 5:33–42.)

Stephen, the first Christian martyr
Stephen was brought before the Jewish council, charged with doing miracles. Stephen told them that they had murdered Jesus, God's special messenger. The council could bear no more. They went out of town, "covered their ears with their hands," and Stephen was stoned to death. Stephen knelt down. His last words were a prayer: "Lord, do not remember this sin against them!"
(See Acts 6:8—8:1.)

Philip the evangelist
Philip, along with Stephen, was one of the extra seven people chosen to help the first apostles. The city of Samaria would never forget Philip's visit. He was an evangelist, preaching to crowds; a healer, stunning people with miracles; and an exorcist, driving out evil spirits from people.
(See Acts 8:4–8.)

The Ethiopian official

The queen of Ethiopia's treasurer was bumping along the dusty road in his elegant chariot. He had a problem. He was trying to puzzle out the meaning of the book of the prophet Isaiah. And then, as if by magic, Philip appeared. What happened was that "the Holy Spirit said to Philip, 'Go over to that chariot.'" Philip told him "the good news about Jesus" and baptized him. (See Acts 8:26–40.)

Jason is roughed up at Thessalonica

Paul and Silas had been staying with a Christian named Jason while they preached in the synagogue at Thessalonica. The Jews became so jealous that they got hold of a rent-a-mob. They caused an uproar in the city, searched for Paul and Silas, and dragged Jason before the authorities in their anger. After paying a fine, Jason was released. He realized how risky it was to help Christian preachers. (See Acts 17:1–9.)

Apollos the preacher

Not all preachers are great speakers. But Apollos was. He was eloquent. He knew his Bible backward and forward and "taught accurately the things of the Lord." (See Acts 18:24–28.)

Demetrius the silversmith

Everything was fine for Demetrius the silversmith. He earned lots of money by making "silver shrines of Diana" in Ephesus. Then Paul spoiled everything by preaching against idol worship. The result? A riot! A great crowd gathered and shouted, "Great is Diana of the Ephesians," for two hours. Paul left town in a hurry! (See Acts 19:21–41.)

Publius's father on Malta

Paul had such an exciting life. He had just been shipwrecked on the island of Malta in the middle of the Mediterranean. Publius, the governor of Malta, looked after Paul for three days. His father was ill in bed with a fever and dysentery. Paul visited him, "prayed, placed his hands on him, and healed him." (See Acts 28:1–10.)

29 THOMAS AND THE TWELVE

The inner three

Peter, James, and John were Jesus' closest disciples. Peter was the leader, always out in front, often speaking before thinking. James and John were brothers and, like Peter, were fishermen. John described himself as "the disciple whom Jesus loved." As Jesus died on the cross, He asked John to look after Mary as if she were his own mother. (See John 19:26–27.)

Andrew

John the Baptist told Andrew that Jesus was "the Lamb of God." Perhaps the best thing Andrew ever did was then. At once he went to get his brother Peter and he introduced him to Jesus. (See John 1:35–42.)

The unknown three

Bartholomew, James (the son of Alphaeus), and Judas (the son of James) were mystery men. We know very little about them!

Philip

During the Last Supper Jesus said, "No one goes to the Father except by Me." Philip did not really understand this, so he asked Jesus to show them the "Father." Jesus replied, "Whoever has seen Me has seen the Father." (See John 14:8–14.)

Matthew

Matthew was a tax collector. When Jesus invited him to follow Him, Matthew left his lucrative business immediately. We remember Matthew as the writer of the first gospel.

"Doubting" Thomas

Thomas got the nickname "doubting" because he refused to believe that Jesus had risen from the dead, even though the other ten disciples had seen Jesus. When, a week later, Thomas did see the risen Jesus, Jesus invited him to put his finger in the wounds in Jesus' hands and his hand in Jesus' wounded side. Thomas believed and said, "My Lord and my God!" (See John 20:24–29.)

Simon the patriot

Before he became Jesus' follower, Simon would have hated Matthew! Matthew worked for the Romans, and Simon worked to overthrow the Romans and send them out of Judea. Simon resented the Romans for occupying his country. That was why he was called Simon the zealot, or Simon the patriot. (See Matthew 10:4.)

Judas the betrayer

Judas Iscariot was treasurer for the 12 disciples. He betrayed Jesus in the Garden of Gethsemane to the chief priests and elders, using a previously arranged signal: "The man I kiss is the one you want. Arrest him!" Judas got 30 pieces of silver for this. In remorse he hanged himself. (See Matthew 26:47–50; Acts 1:18–19.)

30 ZACCHAEUS AND OTHERS WHO MET JESUS

Zacchaeus up in the sycamore tree

Zacchaeus, known locally as the super-rich tax collector, was probably the most unpopular man in Jericho. When Jesus arrived in town, Zacchaeus climbed up a sycamore tree to see Him. Jesus stopped under the tree and invited Himself as a houseguest. Zacchaeus became a new man. He gave back all the money he had cheated people out of and half his wealth to the poor. (See Luke 19:1–10.)

The rich young man

In all the records about Jesus, only one person left in a "very sorrowful" frame of mind. He was a wealthy young man. Jesus challenged him to sell all his possessions and give the money to the poor and follow Him. He could not do it. He went away from Jesus, sad. (See Luke 18:18–30.)

The man with an unclean spirit

The man had many evil spirits in him. He must have been a sight: "Night and day, he was in the mountains and in the tombs, crying out." Jesus cured him by sending the evil spirits into a large herd of pigs, which then rushed down the side of a cliff into the lake and were drowned. (See Mark 5:1–20.)

A 12-year wait

The doctors could do nothing for her, even though she had been seeing them for 12 years. Then she heard about Jesus. Hiding in the crowd she touched His cloak. She thought nobody had seen her. But Jesus had felt power go from Him as she was healed. Jesus told her that her faith had cured her. (See Mark 5:25–34.)

A couple of coins

This person Jesus did not actually meet, but He pointed her out to His disciples. She did not put much into the treasury box: two practically worthless copper coins. Lots of people put in hundreds of times more money than she did. But Jesus said that the poor widow had put the most in. What did He mean? Just that other people had given what they could easily afford, but the widow had put in all she had! (See Mark 12:41–44.)

The man who was blind from Jericho

The man shouted out to Jesus, "Have mercy on me!" "Hush up!" the people hissed. But Jesus called the man to Him, and cured his blindness, telling him that his faith had made him well. Everyone praised God. (See Luke 18:35–43.)

Now you see Him, now you do not!

On the first Easter, two of Jesus' disciples walked from Jerusalem to a village a few miles away called Emmaus. One person was called Cleopas, but we are not told the name of the other person. The risen Lord Jesus walked along with them, but they did not recognize Him. They invited Him in for a meal and He "took some bread and said a blessing over it." And that was when they knew it was Jesus. Then Jesus vanished. (See Luke 24:13–35.)